THE WING

BOOK ABOUT SHAPES WRITTEN AND ILLUSTRATED BY ED EMBERLEY

ON A FLEA

AMMO

A TRIANGLE IS...

A triangle is
The wing on a flea,
And the beak on a bird,
If you'll just look and see.

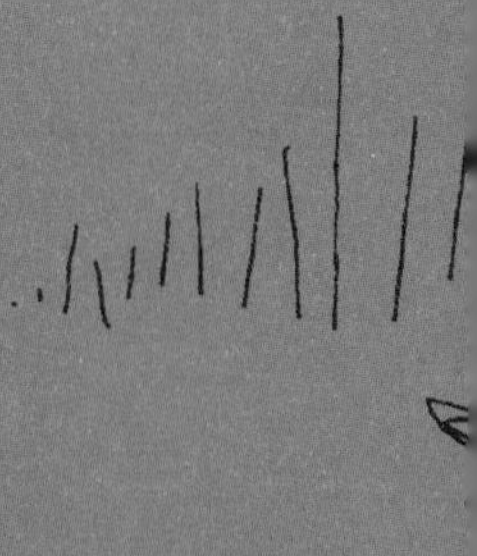

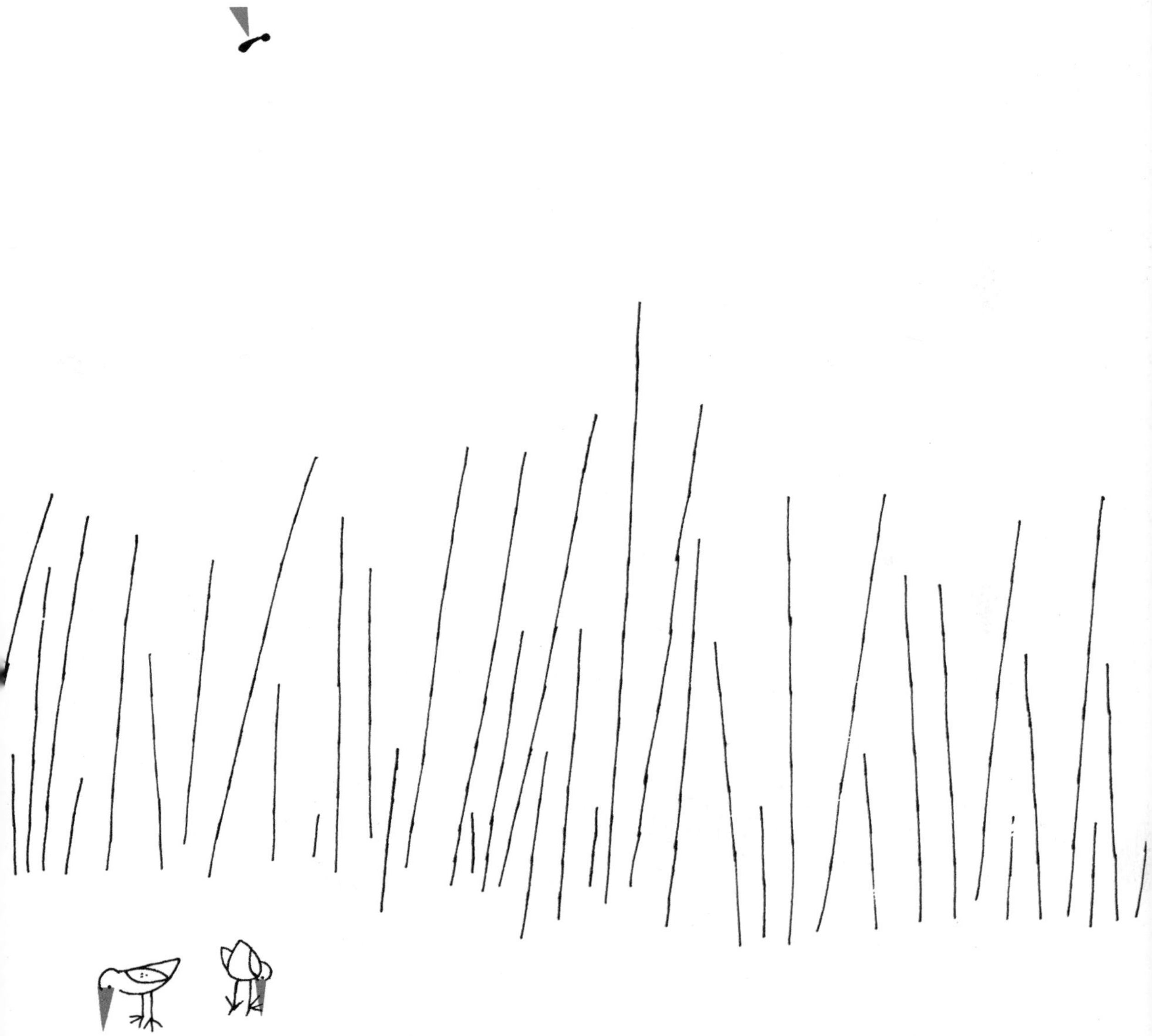

A triangle is
A finny fish-tail,

An ice-cream cone,
A harpoon for a whale,

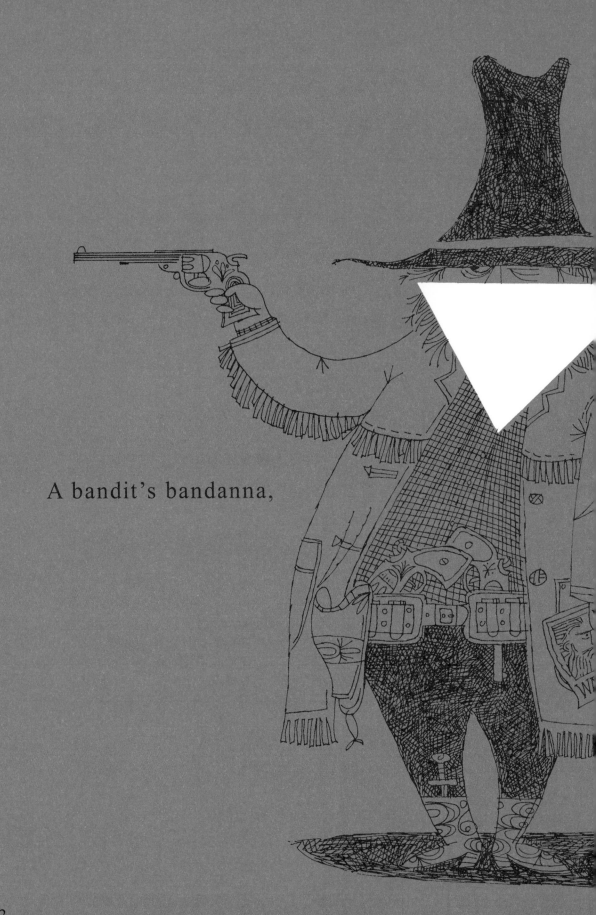

A bandit's bandanna,

An admiral's hat,

And, in case you
don't know it,
The nose on a cat.

It's a sail for a sailor
Who sails on the sea,
A teepee or tree
If you'll just look and see.

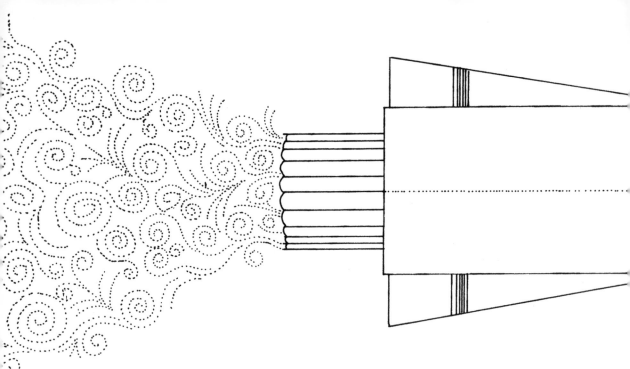

They're as old as the dragons
That knights used to chase,

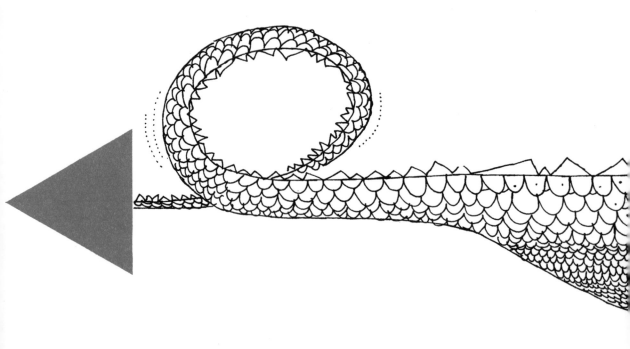

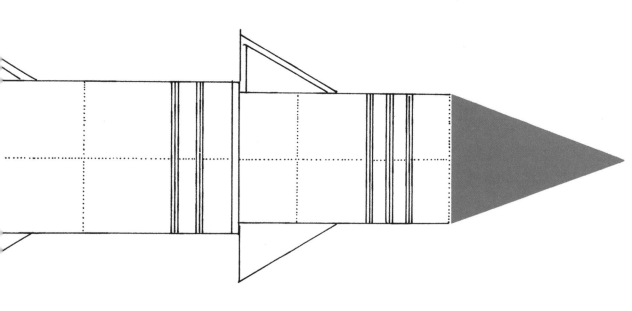

They're as new as the rockets
That shoot into space.

They're as big as a mountain
Or as small as a bee;
You'll find lots around
If you'll just look and see.

A RECTANGLE IS...

A rectangle is,
If you'll just look and see,
A piece of confetti
To throw and say Whee!

A box full of tools

A ruler to measure

And the map pirates use

To find buried treasure.

A rectangle is
A lunch for a goat.
And lots put together
Make a bright, checkered coat.

It's the book you are reading,

It's hopscotch and more...

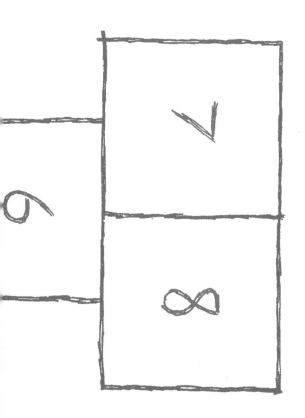

It's the back of a truck,
And the old barn door.

33

It's as small as a house
For a wee chickadee,
Or as big as a skyscraper.
Just look and see!

A CIRCLE IS...

A circle is ⬤
A little green pea,
Or a watering spout,
If you'll just look and see.

A trumpet or drum
To play a fine tune,
A marble, a bubble,
A ball, a balloon.

A circle is
As plain as can be,
A light on a lighthouse
That shines out to sea,

An umbrella you use
For the sun or for rain,
The wheels on a jeep
Or a smoky old train,

The big Ferris wheel
That is so much fun,
The moon and the earth,
And still bigger, the sun.

A circle is
Your eye, which can find
All sorts of shapes.
Now you'll know the kind.

Triangles, rectangles,
Circles, all three,
You'll know which is which
If you just look AND SEE.

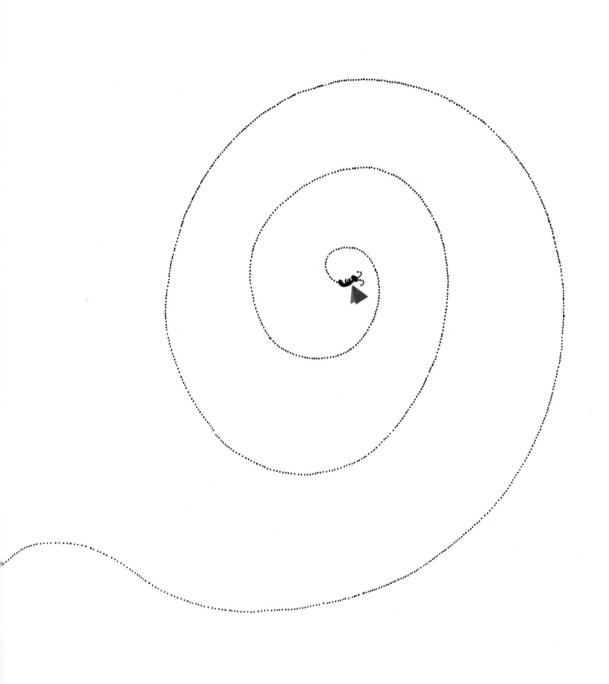

The Wing On A Flea
by Ed Emberley

First Published, 1961

First AMMO Books Edition, 2015

Acquisitions Editor: Gloria Fowler

Production: Megan Shoemaker

Copy Edit: Sara Richmond

Thank you: Rebecca Emberley

ISBN: 9781623260583

Library of Congress Control Number: 2014939834

To enjoy the wonderful world of AMMO Books, please visit us at ammobooks.com.